Debating History

DEBATES ON THE HOLOCAUST

Don Nardo

ReferencePoint Press®

San Diego, CA

© 2019 ReferencePoint Press, Inc.
Printed in the United States

For more information, contact:
ReferencePoint Press, Inc.
PO Box 27779
San Diego, CA 92198
www.ReferencePointPress.com

LIBRARY OF CONGRESS CATALOGING-IN-PUBLICATION DATA

Name: Nardo, Don, 1947–author.
Title: Debates on the Holocaust/by Don Nardo.
Description: San Diego, CA: ReferencePoint Press, [2018] | Series: Debating History series | Grades 9 to 12. | Includes bibliographical references and index.
Identifiers: LCCN 2018020117 (print) | LCCN 2018020822 (ebook) | ISBN 9781682823682 (eBook) | ISBN 9781682823675 (hardback)
Subjects: LCSH: Holocaust, Jewish (1939–1945)—Historiography.
Classification: LCC D804.348 (ebook) | LCC D804.348 .N37 2018 (print) | DDC 940.53/18—dc23
LC record available at https://lccn.loc.gov/2018020117

Contents

Is slavery immoral?

No thinking person today would argue that slavery is moral. Yet in the United States in the early and mid-1800s, slavery was an accepted institution in the southern states. While many southerners never owned slaves, the institution of slavery had widespread support from plantation owners, elected officials, and even the general populace. Its defenders were often respected members of their communities. For instance, John C. Calhoun—a US senator from South Carolina—was a staunch defender of slavery. He believed that enslaved Africans benefited from their status as slaves—and said as much during an 1837 Senate speech. "Never before," he stated, "has the black race of Central Africa, from the dawn of history to the present day, attained a condition so civilized and so improved, not only physically, but morally and intellectually."

Statements like this might be confounding and hurtful today. But a true understanding of history—especially of those events that have altered daily life and human communities—requires students to become familiar with the thoughts, attitudes, and beliefs of the people who lived these events. Only by examining various perspectives will students truly understand the past and be able to make sound judgments about the future.

This is the goal of the *Debating History* series. Through a narrative-driven, pro/con format, the series introduces students to some of the complex issues that have dominated public discourse over the decades—topics such as the slave trade, twentieth-century immigration, the Soviet Union's collapse, and the rise of Islamist extremism. All chapters revolve around a single, pointed question, such as the following:

- Is slavery immoral?
- Do immigrants threaten American culture and values?
- Did the arms race cause the Soviet Union's collapse?
- Does poverty cause Islamist extremism?

This inquiry-based approach to history introduces student researchers to core issues and concerns on a given topic. Each chapter includes one part that argues the affirmative and one part that argues the negative—all written by a single author. With the single-author format, the predominant arguments for and against an issue can be synthesized into clear, accessible discussions supported by details and evidence, including relevant facts, quotes, and examples. All volumes include focus questions to guide students as they read each pro/con discussion, a visual chronology, and a list of sources for conducting further research.

This approach reflects the guiding principles set out in the College, Career, and Civic Life (C3) Framework for Social Studies State Standards developed by the National Council for the Social Studies. "History is interpretive," the framework's authors write. "Even if they are eyewitnesses, people construct different accounts of the same event, which are shaped by their perspectives—their ideas, attitudes, and beliefs. Historical understanding requires recognizing this multiplicity of points of view in the past. . . . It also requires recognizing that perspectives change over time, so that historical understanding requires developing a sense of empathy with people in the past whose perspectives might be very different from those of today." The *Debating History* series supports these goals by providing a solid introduction to the study of pro/con issues in history.

Important Events of the Holocaust

1899
British-born German thinker Houston Stewart Chamberlain publishes the highly anti-Semitic *Foundations of the Nineteenth Century*, which will later strongly influence Adolf Hitler.

1914
World War I begins. The war ends four years later, with Germany's defeat, which Hitler and other Germans blame on the Jews.

1939
In a January speech to Germany's legislature, Hitler predicts the eventual annihilation of Europe's Jews; in September Hitler orders his forces to attack Poland, thereby initiating World War II.

1900 / 1915   1920   1925   1930   1935

1933
Hitler is appointed chancellor of Germany.

1938
On November 9, in the so-called Night of Broken Glass, the Nazis loot more than seven thousand Jewish businesses and arrest some thirty thousand Jews.

1925
Hitler publishes his manifesto *Mein Kampf*, in which he calls for the suppression and elimination of German Jews.

1943
The Jews in the Warsaw Ghetto stage a bloody uprising against their Nazi captors.

1945
Soviet forces liberate the Auschwitz death camp in Poland in January; in April, US soldiers liberate the Dachau death camp in southern Germany; in May, the war in Europe ends; in November, the Nuremberg Trials—in which the chief surviving Nazi leaders are prosecuted by the Allies for war crimes—begin.

1942
An underground Jewish group in the Warsaw Ghetto collects documentation of Nazi extermination of Jews and gets it to London, alerting the world to Hitler's plan.

1940   1941   1942   1943   1944   1945   1946

1940
The Nazis establish the Warsaw Ghetto in Poland, in which large numbers of local Jews are confined.

1944
In June the War Refugee Board requests that the United States and other Allies rescue as many Jews as possible from the Nazi death camps; in July the Emergency Committee to Save the Jewish People of Europe asks US president Franklin D. Roosevelt to bomb the railways leading to the Nazi death camps.

1941
Hitler's forces attacks the Soviet Union in June. In Berlin, in December Hitler and other leading Nazis adopt the Final Solution, the plan to eradicate all Jews from Europe. Germany erects extermination camps primarily to facilitate the genocide.

7

Chapter One

A Brief History of the Holocaust

The Holocaust, which is called *Ha-Shoah* in Hebrew, today refers mainly to the mass murder of Jews by Adolf Hitler's Nazi regime in during World War II (1939–1945). Although members of other groups deemed inferior by the Nazis also died in the Holocaust, the Jews were targeted as a race worthy of extermination because Hitler blamed them for Germany's loss in World War I and considered them vermin who had no national loyalty. Fueled by such falsehoods and hate speech, the Nazis tried to rectify the "problem" of the European Jews by systematically rounding them up and murdering them in staggering numbers. The roughly 6 million Jews who were eradicated by the Nazis represented approximately two-thirds of Europe's Jewish population and one-third of all the world's Jews. Hitler and his minions called the plan to totally rid Europe of Jews the Final Solution.

Fertile Ground for Hate Groups

The Nazis came to power in Germany in the 1930s. They were able to do so in large part because of the negative effects that World War I (1914–1918) had on Germany and its people. Germany lost the war, and the terms imposed on it by its enemies—the Allies—in the Treaty of Versailles were very harsh. The Germans felt victimized and humiliated because they had lost thousands of square miles of territory and had to pay the Allies vast sums of money in the form of war reparations. Germany's fledgling post-war democracy—the Weimar Republic—struggled to stay afloat. This effort became even more difficult when the country entered the worldwide Great Depression brought on by the New York stock market's 1929 crash.

These dire conditions proved to be fertile ground for right-wing hate groups and other antidemocratic forces to grow in. Of these groups, the one that expanded the fastest during the 1920s was Adolf Hitler's Nazi Party. Hitler, who had fought in World War I, was a failed artist and hardened racist who blamed Germany's loss in that conflict on German liberals and bankers and especial-ly the country's Jews. These groups had betrayed the fatherland at home and thereby caused its defeat, he claimed.

Although the Nazis long remained in the minority in Germany, over time their numbers steadily grew, and Hitler managed to gain increasing political attention and power. A major turning point oc-curred in January 1933 when democratic forces in the govern-ment sought to appease him and gain his backing. They appoint-ed him chancellor of Germany, thinking they could control him that way. But this was a grave error. In the months that followed, Hitler used a series of shrewd moves to gain ultimate power over the state. Thereafter, he and his hard-core Nazi lieutenants em-ployed highly effective propaganda tactics to silence their critics and stir up hatred for social groups they disliked.

Social Isolation of the Jews

Chief among those groups were the Jews. From 1934 on, Hitler and his Nazis increasingly vilified and persecuted Jews, blaming them for a host of Germany's ills. According to the Jewish Virtual Library:

The Nazis claimed the Jews corrupted pure German cul-ture with their "foreign" and "mongrel" influence. They portrayed the Jews as evil and cowardly, and Germans as hardworking, courageous, and honest. The Jews, the Nazis claimed, who were heavily represented in finance, commerce, the press, literature, theater, and the arts, had weakened Germany's economy and culture.[1]

Typical among the many elements of the Nazis' anti-Semitic propaganda campaign was the claim that blond, non-Jewish Germans were strong, fit, and moral and thereby destined to rule. In contrast, Jews were portrayed as a weak, racially impure, and morally corrupt people who needed to be isolated from "decent" German society. Books penned by Jews were burned in public bonfires, Jewish teachers were dismissed, Jewish businesses were ransacked, Jewish property was seized, and Jews were often beaten in the streets. This anti-Jewish activity reached its first terrifying zenith on November 9, 1938, in the so-called *Kristallnacht, or* "Night of Broken Glass." More than seven thousand Jewish businesses were looted, dozens of innocent Jews were killed outright, and roughly thirty thousand Jews were arrested and sent to concentration camps.

> "The Nazis claimed the Jews corrupted pure German culture with their "foreign" and "mongrel" influence. They portrayed the Jews as evil and cowardly, and Germans as hardworking, courageous, and honest."[1]
>
> —Jewish Virtual Library

The campaign of isolating Jews from ordinary society accelerated the following year after Hitler attacked Poland, initiating World War II in Europe. In both Germany and Poland, the Nazis rounded up many Jews and consigned them to ghettos, most often parts of cities that had been sectioned off by brick walls or barbed wire. These enclaves did not have enough food, water, sanitation, or medical facilities to decently support the huge numbers of people crowded within them. So numerous Jews died of starvation and disease in the ghettos.

Ghettos, Camps, and Killing Centers, 1942

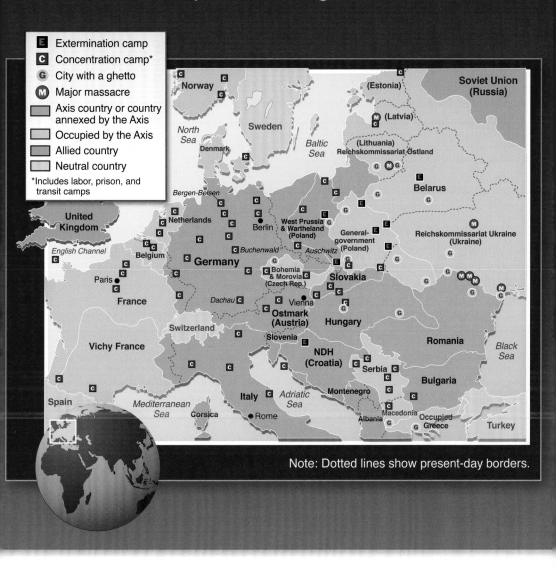

Legend:
- **E** Extermination camp
- **C** Concentration camp*
- **G** City with a ghetto
- **M** Major massacre
- Axis country or country annexed by the Axis
- Occupied by the Axis
- Allied country
- Neutral country

*Includes labor, prison, and transit camps

Note: Dotted lines show present-day borders.

More Efficient Methods of Killing

This dense concentration of Jews in contained areas also helped the Nazis carry out their next escalation of anti-Semitic activity—the Final Solution, in which millions of Jews lost their lives in death camps.

By early 1942 six death camps had sprung up in Poland: Chelmno, Belzec, Sobibor, Treblinka, Maidanek, and Auschwitz. They were purposely situated along railway lines to make it as easy as possible to transport those who were condemned. In addition, a large system of subsidiary camps supported the main death camps. Some were labor camps where Jews and other "undesirables" toiled as literal slaves; others were transit camps designed to hold condemned individuals until it was time to murder them. Some of the camps served both functions.

One thing the commanders of the death camps learned fairly quickly was that killing large numbers of people was time consuming and required considerable manpower. The method of lining up the victims and shooting them down with machine guns had been used in the late 1930s and the first two years of the war. When Germany invaded Russia, killing squads called *Einsatzgruppen* had gathered Jews and others in captured towns, driven them into the countryside, shot them down, and buried them in huge pits. But it became clear that this method was logistically too involved and simply too inefficient to eradicate millions of people.

Nazi leaders soon settled on the use of poison gas as a more efficient and less wasteful method of murder. One of the commanders of the infamous death camp at Auschwitz, Rudolf Hoess, later wrote that he had been ordered in June 1941 to install some kind of effective extermination equipment at Auschwitz. "I visited Treblinka to find out how they carried out their extermination," he recalled.

> The camp commandant at Treblinka told me that he had liquidated 80,000 [people] in the course of half a year. He was principally concerned with liquidating all the Jews from the Warsaw ghetto. He used monoxide gas and I did not think that his methods were very efficient. So when I set up the extermination building at Auschwitz, I used Zyklon B, which was a crystallized prussic acid which we dropped into the death chamber from a small opening. It took from three to fifteen minutes to kill the people in the death chamber, depending upon climatic conditions. We

knew when the people were dead because their scream-
ing stopped. We usually waited about a half hour before
we opened the doors and removed the bodies. After the
bodies were removed, our special commandos took off the
rings and extracted the gold from the teeth of the corpses.
Another improvement we [at Auschwitz] made over Treblinka was that we built our gas chambers to accommodate
2,000 people at one time, whereas at Treblinka their ten
gas chambers only accommodated 200 people each.[2]

In the three years that followed, the Nazis shipped thousands
of Jews to Auschwitz and the other death camps each day. Only
a few hours after arriving at such a camp, new arrivals were
stripped of their valuables and other possessions and gassed to
death. Their bodies were then incinerated in specially designed
crematoriums, or large-scale ovens. Millions of Jews met horrible
ends in this manner.

An Emblem of Barbarity

Eventually, the Western Allies invaded Europe and—with the help
of the Soviet Union—surrounded Nazi Germany and began to
close in on it. As the war steadily ground to its conclusion, the
Nazis dismantled some of the death camps for fear that the victors would find them and punish Germany even more harshly.
Those camps that were not torn down were liberated by American, Soviet, and British forces. Maidanek, for instance, was freed
by the Soviets in July 1944. The Soviets also liberated Auschwitz
in January 1945, while the British seized Bergen-Belsen (near Hanover, Germany) in April 1945. Also in April 1945, the Americans
liberated Dachau (in southern Germany).

The principal perpetrators of the Holocaust paid steep prices
for their crimes against humanity. Realizing that his dream of a
Nazi realm that would last a thousand years had collapsed, Hitler committed suicide in a concrete bunker beneath the streets

"The inhumane conditions and the torturous treatment of the [Jews by the Nazis] only further revealed the true cruelty and brutality behind Hitler's leadership."[3]

—Holocaust Teacher Resource Center

of Berlin just as Soviet troops were entering the city. Several of his Nazi ringleaders did not follow Hitler's form of escape and were tried in the famous Nuremberg Trials following the war. Some were found guilty of war crimes—including genocide—and executed.

As for the Holocaust itself, in the decades following the close of World War II, the enormity of its horrors consistently captured the world's attention. In the fullness of time, that awful event became an emblem of mass barbarity, twisted and sick ideology, and the ultimate in inhumane behavior. As a spokesperson for the online Holocaust Teacher Resource Center puts it:

> When the Allied Forces invaded Germany at the end of World War II, few of the combat veterans were prepared to cope with the horrors they encountered during the liberation of the concentration camps. The inhumane conditions and the torturous treatment of the prisoners only further revealed the true cruelty and brutality behind Hitler's leadership and the reign of the Nazi Party.[3]

Chapter Two

Was Adolf Hitler the Primary Force Behind the Holocaust?

Adolf Hitler Was the Primary Force Behind the Holocaust

- Before Hitler's rise to power, the chief method used against the Jews by anti-Semites was segregation.
- Hitler talked about exterminating the Jews very early in his career, long before meeting many of those who would later become his leading lieutenants.
- Hitler gave the specific order to begin the Final Solution in Munich on December 12, 1941.

The Debate at a Glance

Adolf Hitler Was Not the Primary Force Behind the Holocaust

- Hitler was not an original thinker and did not invent the notion of exterminating Germany's Jews.
- It took Hitler's deputies a while to coordinate their plan to eradicate the Jews because Nazi Germany's government was convoluted and inefficient.
- The Nazi regime was very similar to a religious cult, and like a pope, Hitler needed priest-like deputies to carry out his major policies.

Adolf Hitler Was the Primary Force Behind the Holocaust

"[Hitler] had long-range plans to realize his ideological goals, and the destruction of the Jews was at their center."

—American historian Lucy Dawidowicz

Lucy Dawidowicz, *The War Against the Jews, 1933–1945*. New York: Holt, Rinehart, and Winston, 1975, p. 158.

Consider these questions as you read:

1. Why were Jews frequent targets of hatred and discrimination for many centuries?
2. Why, in your view, do absolute dictators like Hitler typically describe themselves as prophets whose predictions should always be taken seriously?
3. Why would Nazi leaders, including Hitler, be reluctant to commit to paper an order to proceed with genocide?

Editor's note: The discussion that follows presents common arguments made in support of this perspective. All arguments are supported by facts, quotes, and examples taken from various sources of the period or present day.

Many historians and other experts on World War II and Nazi Germany agree that if Adolf Hitler had not risen to power in Germany, the Holocaust would never have come about. Those who argue that he was the primary and guiding force behind the attempted eradication of Europe's Jews are often called intentionalists. This is based on the notion that exterminating the Jews was his intention all along.

From Segregation to Annihilation

That Hitler was the chief guiding force behind the Holocaust is partly proved by the fact that before he came on the scene, the principal approach used against Jews by those who hated them was segregation. Jews had indeed suffered from hatred and discrimination for many centuries. But almost always, anti-Semitic individuals and groups had either banished them or segregated them to "Jewish-only" areas within society. The idea that the Jews should all be exterminated was usually not seriously considered. In the words of a noted expert on the Holocaust, Theodore S. Hamerow:

> While [some anti-Semites believed] the Jews must be treated differently than Christians, they should at least be permitted to lead a separate, semi-autonomous existence, living in their own quarters, following their own customs, obeying their own leaders, and praying in their own houses of worship. The purpose of the restrictions imposed on them was segregation and subordination, not extermination.[4]

In contrast, Hitler formulated a vision of dealing with the Jewish "problem" that went far beyond keeping Jews separate from non-Jews in society. Among his earliest formal written attacks on Jews were those contained in his long, rambling 1925 manifesto *Mein Kampf* (meaning "My Struggle" in German). First, he explained why he viewed Jews as a dangerous criminal element that threatened the very fabric of society. In politics, he said, the Jew

> refuses the state the means for its self-preservation, destroys the foundations of all national self-maintenance and defense, destroys faith in the leadership, scoffs at its history and past, and drags everything that is truly great into the gutter. Culturally, he contaminates art, literature, the theater, makes a mockery of natural feeling, overthrows all concepts of beauty and sublimity, of the noble and the good, and instead drags men down into the sphere of his

own base nature. Religion is ridiculed, ethics and morality represented as outmoded, until the last props of a nation in its struggle for existence in this world have fallen.[5]

Hitler then compared Jews to vampires to emphasize that, like other frightening monsters, there could be no other fate for them but total annihilation. "The end is not only the end of the freedom of the peoples oppressed by the Jew, but also the end of this parasite upon the nations," he wrote. "After the death of his victim, the vampire sooner or later dies too."[6]

> "[The Jew] overthrows all concepts of beauty and sublimity, of the noble and the good."[5]
>
> —Adolf Hitler

No Pity for the Jews

Clearly this reference to killing Jews is an analogy and constitutes more of a general prediction than an organized policy or plan. Yet as the years progressed and Hitler came to power in Germany, his murderous intentions toward the Jews became more pronounced and specific. In January 1939, for example, in a speech he gave to Germany's principal lawmaking body, the Reichstag, he issued a clear warning about how he planned to deal with the Jews. "In the course of my life," he boasted, "I have very often been a prophet and was generally laughed at for it. During my struggle for power, it was in the first instance Jewish people who laughed at my prophecies that I would someday assume the leadership of the state." He added that "their laughter was uproarious," but "for some time now the Jews have been laughing on the other side of their faces. Today I will be a prophet again." It appeared that the Jews were about to plunge humanity into a world war, he said, blaming them in advance for what he himself was about to do. If this happened, he stated in a chilling tone, the result would be "the annihilation of the Jewish race in Europe."[7]

Members of the Reichstag salute Adolf Hitler after he declares war on Poland in 1939. Earlier that same year Hitler alluded to the annihilation of Europe's Jews in a speech before this same body.

By invading Poland later that year, Hitler initiated the most destructive war in history. Moreover, in keeping with his earlier threat to punish the Jews for their supposed role in worsening Germany's fortunes after World War I, he accused them of misdeeds that in reality they had no hand in. He also began explicitly employing the unambiguous and clearly threatening term *exterminate*. On October 25, 1941, he stated, "This race of criminals has the two million dead from the [First] World War on its conscience and now hundreds of thousands more. . . . Who's worrying about our people? It's good if the fear that we are exterminating the Jews goes before us."[8]

Less than a month later, one of Hitler's leading lieutenants, the Nazis' chief propaganda official, Joseph Goebbels, echoed his boss's prediction that the Jews were doomed. "At present we are experiencing the realization of this prophecy [of Hitler's], and in the process Jewry is suffering a fate which may be harsh but is more than deserved. Pity or regret is entirely inappropriate in this case."[9]

Black-and-White Documentation

The long series of references that Hitler made to "exterminating" or "annihilating" the Jews between the early 1920s and early 1940s strongly suggests that he had conceived of killing them fairly early in his adulthood. This was long before he had even met most of the men who later became his most prominent followers. So it seems certain that he was the primary force behind the conception of that dastardly plan to commit mass murder.

To be sure of this beyond the shadow of a doubt, one would require some sort of black-and-white documentation. To that end, historians have long searched for a memo or some other sort of written order in which Hitler clearly directed one or more subordinates to do the deed. No single directive of that nature has yet been uncovered, however. It may someday be found, of course. But as a number of experts have pointed out, Hitler may well have deliberately refrained from creating such a document. After all, in the unlikely event (in his mind) that the Allies won the war, he would not have wanted to provide them with powerful proof of his attempt to commit genocide.

Instead, it is more probable that the directive in question was delivered verbally. Northwestern University scholar Peter Hayes thinks that this verbal order was given on December 12, 1941, the day after Hitler declared war on the United States (to match a similar declaration against the Americans made by his ally, Japan). On that day he met with around fifty of his chief lieutenants in his private apartment in Munich. No known written record was kept of the meeting. But the next day Goebbels made an entry in his diary that confirms that the men discussed the Jews' ultimate fate. "With respect of the Jewish Question," Goebbels said, Hitler

> is determined to clean the table. He prophesized that should the Jews once again bring about a world war, they would be annihilated. These were no empty words. The world war has come, therefore the annihilation of the Jews has to be its inevitable consequence. The question has to be examined without any sentimentality. We are not here to pity Jews, but to have pity for our own German people. If the German people have sacrificed about 160,000 dead in the battles in the east, the instigators of this bloody conflict will have to pay for it with their lives.[10]

The phrases "clean the table," "the annihilation of the Jews," and "pay for it with their lives" in Goebbels' journal, though secondhand remarks made after the fact, are clear enough. This shows that the order to begin what would later be called the Holocaust came directly from Hitler. Further evidence takes the form of a remark made by German diplomat Otto Bräutigam five days later, on December 18, 1941. "As for the Jewish question," he stated, "oral discussions have taken place [and] have brought about clarification."[11] The "oral discussions" mentioned here are almost surely a reference to the December 12 meeting in Munich. It cannot be a coincidence that within a few months of that gathering, the gas chambers began to be installed in several of the death camps.

"We are not here to pity Jews, but to have pity for our own German people."[10]

—Nazi propaganda minister Joseph Goebbels

21

Adolf Hitler Was Not the Primary Force Behind the Holocaust

"Hitler's heightened rhetoric prompted others to realize his 'utopian' ravings about Jews and undoubtedly stimulated murderous excesses. But he issued no order for the Final Solution and had nothing to do with its implementation."

—Canadian historian Michael R. Marrus

Michael R. Marrus, *The Holocaust in History*. Hanover, NH: University Press of New England, 1987, p. 42.

Consider these questions as you read:

1. In your view, why would Nazi leaders, including Hitler, want to project a "strong Hitler" image to both Germans and foreigners?
2. When listing the supposed economic powers the Jews possessed, Nazi leaders routinely failed to mention Jewish contributions to society. What were some of those contributions?
3. How did singling out the Jews as targets of ridicule and scorn help Hitler gain and then maintain political power in Germany?

Editor's note: The discussion that follows presents common arguments made in support of this perspective. All arguments are supported by facts, quotes, and examples taken from various sources of the period or present day.

The intentionalists—those historians and other scholars who argue that Hitler conceived the Holocaust largely on his own and specifically ordered its initiation—are incorrect because they ignore another, more convincing body of evidence. As the thinkers known as the functionalists, or structuralists, stress, Hitler was *not* the prime architect of the extermination of Europe's Jews. First, Hitler lacked several of the strong leadership qualities he would have needed both to conceive and carry out an effective extermination plan. This is partly because he was a poor planner and made most of his decisions on the spur of the moment. He was also unpredictable rather than firm and thoughtful.

In fact, the whole idea that Hitler was a dominating, strong-willed leader who commanded both the Nazi Party and Germany with an iron fist is largely a myth. Instead, that "strong Hitler" theory is based mainly on Nazi propaganda rather than reality. Hitler was definitely an anti-Semite. But most of the time he acted to appease the even more hard-line anti-Semites in the Nazi administration. It was a group of his deputies, a number of hard-core, lifelong Jew haters, who constituted the primary force behind the Holocaust.

Hitler's Idea Not Original

Hitler wrote about the possibility of killing the Jews as far back as the early 1920s. Yet even then it was far from an original idea. Germany and other European countries had churned out anti-Jewish literature for centuries, and some of it was laced with threats—sometimes veiled and sometimes not—against Jewish life and limb. One of the most influential of these writings appeared in 1899. Titled *The Foundations of the Nineteenth Century*, its author was a widely popular British-born German thinker named Houston Stewart Chamberlain.

Chamberlain held that Jews were the scum of the earth and human society, both of which would be far better without them. In his book he stated, "The men who founded Judaism

> "The Jews' existence is sin, their existence is a crime against the holy laws of life."[12]
>
> —British-born German thinker Houston Stewart Chamberlain

were goaded on by a demoniacal [Satanic] power. The Jews' existence is sin, their existence is a crime against the holy laws of life. Not only the Jew, but also all that is derived from the Jewish mind, corrodes and disintegrates what is best in us."[12]

Since the very existence of the Jews was a sin, Chamberlain reasoned, their nonexistence should be firmly promoted by the leaders of "decent" society. Not only Hitler but also his chief deputies, including his propaganda minister, Joseph Goebbels, were highly influenced by the works of Chamberlain and other writers who agreed that Jews posed a danger to society. Therefore, those deputies did not need Hitler to teach them to be anti-Semitic and to desire to eradicate Jews.

In fact, Hitler was far from the deep, original thinker he imagined himself to be. Rather, his intellectual foundations were quite shallow, and his views of the world and the workings of cause and effect were fairly simplistic. For him, his deep hatred of Jews was a good enough reason to want to segregate and punish them. Ultimately, he believed Germany would be better off without any Jews, and he would have been glad to see them all banished to Russia or anywhere else.

In contrast, some Nazi leaders *did* give fairly extensive thought to the so-called Jewish problem. In the short run, they reasoned, kicking the Jews out of Germany might be a useful approach. But at some point in the future, leading Nazis hoped, Germany would conquer large portions of the globe. Sooner or later, therefore, they would once again encounter those Jews they had exiled. What then? Would the Jews still pose a threat to Germany's interests, and if so, what would be the benefit of exiling them once more? Hitler's deputies concluded that there was, in both the near term and the more distant future, an economic incentive to eliminating large numbers of Jews. According to Regis College historian Vera Laska:

Germany greatly profited from the elimination of the Jews, whose confiscated properties became the bounties of the Germans. [They included] real estate [and] businesses and homes, stocks and bonds, bank deposits and liquid assets, jewelry and art objects, even the clothes from the Jews' backs and the gold from their teeth. The people who did the [oral] extractions in Auschwitz testified in detail how the gold

24

crowns and fillings were salvaged from the corpses on their way from the gas chambers to the crematoria. German racial propaganda repeatedly touched upon the economic power of the Jews (omitting their contributions). Thus, the largest mass robbery in history was glazed with lofty sounding theories and provided a "moral" excuse for criminal acts.[13]

On the Path to Genocide

It is important to emphasize that the actual initiation of Nazi Germany's policy of Jewish extermination did not happen all at once—through a direct order from Hitler—as often portrayed by intentionalist writers. The fact is that the high-placed Nazis who implemented the Holocaust were not very well organized and took months and even years to coordinate their anti-Jewish plans. According to British documentarian Laurence Rees, "Some people had decided that, because the crime of the extermination of the Jews was so horrendous, it must have been orchestrated and planned at one monumental moment. But [this] was a mistaken leap. [The] journey to the Holocaust was a gradual one, full of twists and turns."[14]

Some experts refer to those twists and turns on the path to genocide as the "crooked path" to the Holocaust. It is based partly on the reality that the apparatus of the Nazi regime was what University of Toronto professor emeritus Michael R. Marrus calls "a bureaucratic and administrative jungle." In Hitler's Nazi government, he explains, "office was piled upon office and underlings were left to find their way." The only useful "guide to success, and a compelling one, was fidelity to the Hitlerian vision. Underlings competed for the favor of this ideologically obsessed, but essentially lazy leader."[15]

Thus, Hitler certainly raved on and on about how inferior the Jews were and the need to do something about them. But he issued no specific order to begin the Final Solution. Instead, he made it clear that he wanted something done about the Jews and left it up to his closest lieutenants to formulate and implement a workable plan.

The Hitlerian Cult

Indeed, considering how unoriginal and untalented Hitler was as a leader (although he *was* a gifted public speaker who could sway a crowd), he desperately needed these deputies. Only their political and administrative contributions could make his entire power structure function with any degree of success. Nazi Germany—including its international conquests and anti-Jewish brutalities—was, for all intents and purposes, a new form of national religion. In that analogy, Hitler was the pope or archbishop who required an army of priests to support him. As Pulitzer Prize–winning historian Richard Rhodes says, "Hitler's dazzling rise to power and the charismatic [magnetic] authority his millions of followers ceded to him,

Adolf Hitler is surrounded in this photograph by various senior military officers and aides. These and other individuals provided the crucial political and administrative know-how that Hitler lacked.

derive directly from the religion-like structure of his politics; National Socialism as Hitler organized it was essentially a religious cult."[16]

It is hardly surprising, therefore, that one of the foundations of Hitler's cult—extreme anti-Jewish hatred—found its highest expression not in Hitler but in several of his deputies. Sociologists and other scientists have documented this sort of approach to national policy repeatedly. Dictators like Hitler invariably surround themselves with hard-core loyal followers who agree with both their prejudices and central aims. Such prejudices are usually aimed at one or more specific groups within society. In the words of French philosopher René Girard:

> Suddenly the opposition of everyone against everyone is replaced by the opposition of all against one. Where previously there had been a chaotic ensemble of particular conflicts, there is now the simplicity of a single conflict. The entire community [is] on one side, and on the other [is] the victim. The nature of this sacrificial resolution is not difficult to comprehend. The community finds itself unified once more at the expense of a victim.[17]

In Nazi Germany, the Jews became that societal victim. It was not just Hitler deciding how to hurt the Jews; it was also a number of like-minded followers. They took it upon themselves to figure out ways in which to rid Germany of what they, along with their boss, viewed as inferiors. Eventually, Hitler's advisers made it clear that various technical means existed to exterminate Jews on a mass scale. At that juncture, they made the complete eradication of the Jews available to Hitler as an option—and he took that option. But the plan was initially theirs, not his, and on his behalf they proceeded to implement it.

> "National Socialism as Hitler organized it was essentially a religious cult."[16]
>
> —Historian Richard Rhodes

Chapter Three

Could Europe's Jews Have Put Up More Resistance to Nazi Aggression?

Europe's Jews Failed to Resist Nazi Aggression

- The Jews lacked the organization they needed to mount an effective resistance.
- In place of armed resistance, most Jews substituted petitions, bribery, and working hard for their oppressors.
- The Jews did not resist in part because it was difficult for them to believe that the leaders of a civilized nation could commit genocide.

The Debate at a Glance

Europe's Jews Resisted Nazi Aggression as Forcefully as They Could

- In European ghettos, Jews secretly collected information about conditions there and smuggled it to the Allies.
- A number of Jews escaped from ghettos and work camps and joined resistance groups in the countryside.
- Sometimes Jews living in ghettos and even the death camps rose up and fought back against their captors.

Europe's Jews Failed to Resist Nazi Aggression

"The [Nazis'] bureaucratic machine, operating with accelerating speed and ever-widening destructive effect, proceeded to annihilate the European Jews. The Jewish community, unable to switch to resistance, increased its cooperation with the tempo of the German measures, thus hastening its own destruction."

—Austrian-born American historian Raul E. Hilberg

Raul E. Hilberg, *The Destruction of the European Jews*, vol. 1. New York: Holmes and Meier, 1985, p. 27.

Consider these questions as you read:

1. Hitler began stirring up hatred for Jews long before the Holocaust. What crimes and unpatriotic plots did he attribute to them in the immediate wake of World War I?
2. Many people around the world were surprised that a cultured nation like Germany became the perpetrator of genocide. What were some of the scientific, artistic, and other German advances of the late 1800s and early 1900s?
3. How did Nazi plans to exterminate millions of Jews work against Germany's own best interests?

Editor's note: The discussion that follows presents common arguments made in support of this perspective. All arguments are supported by facts, quotes, and examples taken from various sources of the period or present day.

During the 1930s and 1940s, Nazi Germany exploited, oppressed, and ultimately murdered millions of German and other European Jews. In the course of those years, the vast majority of Jews did not offer significant physical resistance. Indeed, as a rule they complied with their oppressors' orders and hoped for the best, even as they were being systematically slaughtered.

> "In reality [the Jews] had no organization of their own at all. . . . If they had had some sort of organization, these people could have been saved by the millions."[19]
>
> —Nazi officer Erich von dem Bach

According to Raul Hilberg, a noted historian of the Holocaust, "The reaction pattern of the Jews [was] characterized by almost complete lack of resistance."[18]

Hilberg and the scholars who agree with him base that assertion partly on direct observations by the very Nazis who dealt with the Jews on a regular basis. According to a leading Nazi officer, Erich von dem Bach, "The mass of the Jewish people were taken completely by surprise" when the Nazis herded them into ghettos and then transferred them to concentration and death camps.

> They did not know at all what to do. They had no directives or slogans as to how they should act. That is the greatest lie of anti-Semitism because it gives the lie to the slogan that the Jews are conspiring to dominate the world and that they are so highly organized. In reality they had no organization of their own at all, not even an information service. If they had had some sort of organization, these people could have been saved by the millions. [Never] before has a people gone as unsuspectingly to its disaster.[19]

Various Nonviolent Approaches

Thus, instead of staging armed rebellions and other means of direct physical resistance across Germany and neighboring nations, the Jews tended to react in other ways. In the 1930s, during the earliest stages of Nazi anti-Jewish oppression, Jewish leaders employed the tactic of pleading, usually in the form of petitions. Redressing grievances by bringing petitions to local or national leaders had a long, distinguished history in Europe among both Jews and non-Jews. So when Hitler and his Nazis began curtailing Jewish rights in

Germany, elders of local Jewish communities assumed that drawing up petitions of grievances was the logical first step to take. There was a widespread hope, at least at first, that Nazi leaders would look at those grievances and seriously consider addressing them.

When petitions did not work, the Jews tried other nonviolent means of dealing with Nazi subjugation. One was bribing Nazi soldiers and guards. "Typical," Hilberg writes, "were offers for the release of forced laborers or a ransom of Jews about to be shot."[20] This approach proved successful in only a few isolated instances, however, and at best saved a handful of Jewish lives.

More effective, at least some of the time, was for Jews to work as hard as possible for their Nazi captors. The hope was that first, doing this would make Jews seem useful, even indispensable, to the Nazi regime. Second, some Jews reasoned that as long as they were gainfully working, they were alive, and sooner or later the Allies would win the war and liberate them before things got any worse.

Jews work in a saddle-making workshop in the Polish city of Lodz in 1940. Some Jews hoped to escape the Nazi death camps by working hard and demonstrating their usefulness to their captors.

A State of Disbelief

It is only natural to wonder why European Jews of the 1930s and 1940s reacted to Nazi oppression and mass murder chiefly in these nonviolent ways. Of the several reasons, one of the more important was a general and earnest refusal on the part of many Jews to believe that the Nazi authorities were committing large-scale mass murder. It was extremely difficult for most Jews to accept that Germany's leaders could be so irrational and cruel. For one thing, Germany had long been seen as one of the world's most advanced and civilized nations. Also, it made no sense for the Nazis to indiscriminately slaughter the Jews, who were providing them with hugely valuable wartime labor.

Therefore, most Jews simply did not believe the rumors of death camps that now and then filtered into Jewish communities. Some idea of this attitude can be seen in a writing left behind by Calel Perechodnik, a Jew who lived for a while in the Polish town of Otwock. In 1942 he and his companions heard a rumor that Nazi henchmen had gathered fourteen thousand Jews in a Polish town square and mowed them all down with machine guns. "Is it possible to believe such a thing?" Perechodnik asked.

> To shoot without reason women, innocent children just like that in full daylight? After all, even the worst female criminal cannot be sentenced to death if she is pregnant—and here they apparently killed small children. Where can you find people, fathers of families, who would have the courage to aim their machine guns at helpless, small children? Where is the opinion of the cultured world? [It] is probably not true.[21]

Perechodnik went on to describe another rumor about a town in which twenty thousand Jews were supposedly shot to death by Nazi troops. If this was true, he said, it had to be because they "were Soviet citizens and probably because they fought against the Germans." He added, "But we are citizens of the General Government [the German occupation], [so] such a thing cannot happen here."[22]

Masters of Deception

Another reason why most European Jews of the period in question did not resist when they had the chance was that the Nazis were masters of deception. Most of the mass killings of Jews occurred before they realized they were on the verge of death. The Nazis who designed the death camps and carried out the slaughter were diabolical, inhumane individuals who had thought out the process well in advance. To ensure that it would run as smoothly as possible, they employed several ruses, some of them fairly elaborate.

For example, Jews who were herded into boxcars destined for a death camp were commonly told they were headed for a work camp. That way there would likely be no violent resistance on the train. When the captives arrived at their destination, other lies and deceptions awaited them, these too designed to lessen the probability of resistance. At the Treblinka camp, for example, the Nazis built a fake railway station complete with convincing details. These included a uniformed ticket collector, signs bearing the names of other destinations in Poland, and the false front of a restaurant. Those and many similar touches gave the Jews the impression that they had arrived in an ordinary town; in comparison, people expected that a death camp would feature no amenities for travelers. Hence, most Jews who ended up at Treblinka had no idea what was about to happen to them, so they did not resist.

Israeli historian Eric Gartman explains what typically happened after the prisoners exited a train's boxcars:

An immaculately dressed Nazi guard would address the crowd and apologize for the inconveniences they had experienced. He would promise them a better life in the work camps, where they could live together with their families. Food and quarters would be plentiful, much better than in the ghettoes. He would tell them they needed to disinfect from the long journey. Changing quarters complete with hooks for clothing and a cashier's booth where they were handed receipts were provided. It all seemed in order.[23]

No Way to Unlearn an Old Lesson

There were other reasons why most Jews did not resist the Nazis who were trying to exterminate them. For instance, most Jews who had been forced into ghettos to await trains to the death camps lacked the weapons they would have required to wage a successful struggle. Other reasons for not resisting varied from situation to situation.

But whatever the reasons, the upshot was always the same. The condemned Jews largely complied with whatever orders the Nazis gave them. They seemed to hope that their oppressors would ultimately not go too far—certainly not as far as mass murder on an unprecedented scale. "This hope was founded on a 2,000-year experience," Hilberg explains.

> "The Jews had always been a minority, always in danger, but they had learned that they could avert or survive destruction by placating and appeasing their enemies."[24]
>
> —Historian Raul Hilberg

> In exile, the Jews had always been a minority, always in danger, but they had learned that they could avert or survive destruction by placating and appeasing their enemies. [They believed that] armed resistance in the face of overwhelming force could end only in disaster. Thus, over a period of centuries the Jews had learned that in order to survive they had to refrain from resistance. [Only] in 1942, 1943, and 1944, did the Jewish leadership realize that, unlike the [persecutions] of past centuries, the modern machine-like destruction process would engulf European Jewry. But the realization came too late. A 2,000-year-old lesson could not be unlearned. The Jews could not make the switch. They were helpless.[24]

Europe's Jews Resisted Nazi Aggression as Forcefully as They Could

"The activities of the [Jewish] resistance were infinite. Planning and carrying them out involved thousands of women, men, and even children."

—Vera Laska, Regis College historian

Vera Laska, *Women in the Resistance and in the Holocaust: The Voices of Eyewitnesses*. Westport, CT: Greenwood, 1983, p. 4.

Consider these questions as you read:

1. If you had been a German Jew in the mid- to late 1930s, would you have moved to another country or stayed and resisted the Nazis? Why?
2. If you had lived in the Warsaw ghetto (or another Jewish ghetto) during World War II, would you have joined the uprising? Why or why not?
3. Was bombing French restaurants, warehouses, and trains in order to weaken the Nazi occupiers morally justified? Why or why not?

Editor's note: The discussion that follows presents common arguments made in support of this perspective. All arguments are supported by facts, quotes, and examples taken from various sources of the period or present day.

The charge that the Jews oppressed by the Nazis in World War II almost never offered physical resistance is blatantly wrong. In the words of Open University scholar Lyn Smith:

> Although starvation, exposure, and disease sapped the strength and the will of many [Jewish] ghetto inmates to act, Jews did resist, through a range of actions. This included

their refusal to surrender their humanity and personal integrity, to daring escapes and going into hiding, ghetto uprisings, and revolts. Even in the [death] camps, sabotage and incidents of defiance occurred. There were, therefore, many kinds of Jewish resistance.[25]

Indeed, Jewish resistance against the Nazis was extremely widespread and common in Germany and Poland, as well as in neighboring regions the Nazis conquered. Although in the collective sense these bold acts were not enough to save the many Jews whom the Nazis did murder, an undetermined number of potential victims—thousands at least—survived the war thanks to Jewish resistance of various kinds. "The activities of the resistance" were far too many to count, historian Vera Laska states. She explains:

Planning and carrying them out involved thousands of women, men, and even children. Resisters came from all walks of life, from princes and paupers, and they served as messengers, couriers, typists, writers, editors, guides, chauffeurs, pilots, nurses, doctors, radio operators, cipher [code-breaking] clerks, artists, photographers, saboteurs, experts on explosives, and forgers of documents and ration coupons.[26]

Alerting the Allies

Not all these resisters employed overtly violent means. As Smith says, some resisted by managing to stay alive under the most dehumanizing conditions imaginable. Others, in addition, involved themselves in covert, or secret, activities. These were intended to save Jews and others by obstructing the Nazi war effort and, conversely, strengthening the hand of the Allies against the Nazis.

For example, in the biggest of the Jewish ghettos the Nazis created—in Warsaw, Poland—an underground Jewish group formed. Known as *Oneg Shabbat*, or OS for short, its goal was to secretly collect large amounts of information about the awful conditions in the ghetto and somehow get that knowledge to the Allies, encouraging them to act and save what remaining Jews they could. Early in 1942 the OS smuggled a treasure trove of documents outside the Warsaw Ghetto, and this data eventually reached London. One of the OS activists, Emmanuel Ringelblum, recorded with pride in his diary:

> The OS group has fulfilled a great historical mission. It has alarmed the world to our fate, and perhaps saved hundreds of thousands of Polish Jews from extermination. [I] do not know who of our group will survive, who will be deemed worthy to work through our collected material. But one thing is clear to all of us. Our toils and tribulations, our devotions and constant terror, have not been in vain. We have struck the enemy a hard blow.[27]

Unfortunately for Ringelblum and his fellow conspirators, the British government did not immediately act on the information it received from the OS. At the time, Britain itself was under direct Nazi attack, and British leaders felt there was little they could do to help the Warsaw Jews. Nevertheless, as scholar Michael R. Marrus points out, "one can hardly deny the resistance goals of Ringelblum and his group, and one can hardly challenge their authenticity in pursuing them."[28]

"Our toils and tribulations, our devotions and constant terror, have not been in vain. We have struck the enemy a hard blow."[27]

—Jewish resistance fighter Emmanuel Ringelblum

Resisters in the Countryside

More overt were the many instances of Jews successfully escaping the ghettos, work camps, and other places of captivity

> "With their bare hands they pulled down telephone poles and ripped out telegraph wires. . . . They removed bolts from train rails and laid explosives under the tracks that had taken their loved ones to death."[29]
>
> —Researcher Doreen Rappaport

and fighting the Nazis from hiding places in the countryside. The escapees were of all ages and came from all walks of life. Usually, upon breaking free of Nazi control, they either joined or formed their own groups of guerilla fighters. They acted as snipers, picking off individual German soldiers; destroyed train tracks and bridges to slow down enemy troop and supply transports; forged documents for members of the resistance; and ran underground newspapers. The resisters carried out these daring activities even though they were vastly "outnumbered" and "out-armed," researcher Doreen Rappaport writes.

In the dark of night they wrapped their feet in rags and forded rivers and traipsed through forests and over mountains to ambush the enemy. With their bare hands they pulled down telephone poles and ripped out telegraph wires. They planted homemade explosives under bridges and granaries and communications systems. They removed bolts from train rails and laid explosives under the tracks that had taken their loved ones to death. Then they looked for the explosion of light and sound that marked their triumph.[29]

Some of the escapees and resistance fighters became widely known for their courage and skill as warriors. After Hitler launched his attack on the Soviet Union in June 1941, a number of Jews from Soviet towns joined the underground. Among them was Hana Ginzberg, whom all members of the anti-Nazi Soviet underground respected and praised. Another Jewish member of the

Soviet resisters, Valdimir Epshtyn, was captured by Nazis and sent to die at Auschwitz. But he and two fellow Soviets escaped and made it to a remote forest near Krakow, Poland. There they established a renowned resistance group that over time killed some 120 Nazi soldiers.

The Ghetto Uprisings

When possible, the escapees who fought in the underground resistance also devoted time and energy to aiding uprisings that took part in the very ghettos in which they had once lived. Such rebellions occurred in the ghettos of Bialystok, Krakow, Bedzin-Sosnowiec, and Warsaw, all in Nazi-occupied Poland. Biggest of all was the revolt that took place in Warsaw in 1943. Between July and September 1942, German soldiers had removed several thousand Jews from the ghetto and put them on trains bound for work and death camps. No significant resistance occurred at this

Jewish residents of the Warsaw Ghetto are pulled from their hiding places during the 1943 uprising. Despite facing violent Jewish resistance, the heavily armed Nazis crushed the rebellion.

point, so the Nazis were not prepared for what happened later.

In January 1943 German troops reentered the ghetto, intending once again to round up several thousand of the inhabitants. Only this time the soldiers found themselves under attack. Taken by surprise, the Nazis retreated beyond the barricades. Not until a few months later, in mid-April, did they go back in, and once again they encountered violent resistance. For twenty-seven days the Jews lobbed bombs at the soldiers, as well as fired guns they had taken from dead Nazis or obtained from the outside resistance. The heavily armed Germans did prevail, scholar Peter Longerich points out, but only

> by using explosives and incendiary devices, moving from house to house, and hiding place to hiding place. Despite putting up tremendous resistance, the [remaining Jews] were wiped out, except for a small number who were able to escape. Apart from this, thousands of ghetto-dwellers were killed during the fighting. The survivors were deported either to the gas chambers of Treblinka or the labor camps. Their attackers suffered several dozen fatalities.[30]

Resistance in the Cities

Jews also resisted the Nazis in the cities, using homemade bombs whenever possible. This happened all over Nazi-occupied Europe, but some of the more dramatic examples occurred in France. There, the *Francs-Tireurs et Partisans* ("Free-Shooters and Partisans"), or FTP, an extensive underground movement of both Jews and non-Jews, stealthily infiltrated Paris and other urban areas.

FTP's Jewish unit in Paris consisted of about forty men and women, including Abraham Lissner, who survived the war and published a memoir about his Nazi-fighting experiences. He described how German secret police constantly hunted for resisters like him. But members of the FTP were extremely careful to make themselves look as unassuming as possible. After pretending to be ordinary French workers for weeks and months at a time, suddenly they would strike, hitting the enemy hard.

Lissner scored a major achievement for the group on August 11, 1942, when he placed a powerful bomb outside a hotel restaurant frequented by Nazi officers. There were many other similar successes. Lissner later estimated that in less than two years his unit alone bombed nineteen hotels and thirteen warehouses, derailed numerous trains, and killed upward of three thousand Nazis.

Movingly capturing the courageous spirit of the many Jewish resisters across Europe was a patriotic song composed in 1943 to honor them. Titled "Never Say This Is the Final Road for You," its lyrics, by Lithuanian Jew Hirsh Glick, were inspired by the bravery of the Warsaw Ghetto's resistance fighters. It begins, "Never say that this is the end of the road. Wherever a drop of our blood fell, there our courage will grow anew. This song, written in blood, was sung by a people fighting for life and freedom. Our triumph will come and our resounding footsteps will proclaim 'We are here!'"[31]

Chapter Four

Could the Allies Have Reduced the Severity of the Holocaust?

The Allies Could Have Reduced the Severity of the Holocaust

- In 1944 American Jewish leaders urged President Franklin D. Roosevelt to try to save as many European Jews as possible.
- Rescuing as many Jews as possible was the morally right thing to do.
- A number of rescue plans were possible, among them bombing the death camps and making secret deals with leading Nazis.

The Debate at a Glance

The Allies Could Not Have Reduced the Severity of the Holocaust

- The death camps in Poland were too far away for Allied bombers to reach without taking huge risks.
- Anti-Semitic feelings were strong enough in the West to dissuade leaders from making the rescue of European Jews a priority.
- There was real worry among Allied leaders that rescuing the Jews would initiate a huge flood of refugees into Western nations.

The Allies Could Have Reduced the Severity of the Holocaust

"Not another hour [should] be lost in rescuing from the lands in the hands of Hitler the remaining Jews!"

—American Jewish leader Stephen S. Wise

Stephen S. Wise, *As I See It*. New York: Jewish Opinion, 1944, p. 77.

Consider these questions as you read:

1. In your view, would it have been morally right or wrong for the Allies to bomb German civilians until the Jews were released from the death camps? Explain your answer.
2. During the war some Americans felt the Allies were to blame for Nazi excesses because they did not act to contain Hitler's ambitions during the 1930s. Do you agree or disagree? Explain your answer.
3. Do you feel that the Americans and British made a mistake in not accepting the Europa Plan? Why or why not?

Editor's note: The discussion that follows presents common arguments made in support of this perspective. All arguments are supported by facts, quotes, and examples taken from various sources of the period or present day.

No historian or other expert on the Holocaust thinks that the Allied nations could have totally stopped that awful slaughter from happening once World War II had commenced. In the conflict's initial two to three years, the Allies did know that the Nazis had herded millions of Jews into urban ghettos and various kinds of concentration camps. But during that period the information the Allies received about mass extermination of Jews was sketchy and mostly in the form of rumors. Also, when those rumors were eventually substantiated, midway through the war, the Allies lacked the means of completely halting the mass murders in the death camps.

However, many experts agree that the Allies could at least have reduced the severity of the Holocaust well before the end of the conflict. In the postwar years various historians and other interested individuals have addressed the question of why more was not done to try to stop the Nazi Jewish genocide. One noted scholar of the Holocaust asks:

Why couldn't the Allies negotiate with the German government to release Jews in the death camps in return for financial inducements or economic concessions? Why couldn't they announce that the air raids destroying German cities would continue and increase until the genocide had stopped? And, most important, why couldn't they bomb the railroad tracks leading to the death camps or the death camps themselves? Some of the prisoners would undoubtedly have been killed, but not nearly so many as died in the course of a slow, orderly, methodical process of ethnic extermination.[32]

Atoning for a Past Failure

Although those words were written well after the war was over, even during the conflict some concerned individuals in the United States, Britain, and elsewhere called on their leaders to act. Saving at least some German and other European Jews was not only possible but also imperative, they asserted. Early in 1944, for example, American Jewish leader Stephen S. Wise said there was no time to waste, because the Nazis were killing Jews each and every day. "Any further delay of rescue," he exclaimed, "would doubtless mean that there would be no Jews to save in what was Hitler's Europe."[33]

> "Any further delay of rescue would doubtless mean that there would be no Jews [left] to save."[33]
>
> —American Jewish leader Stephen S. Wise

The reason the United States and other Allies should rescue however many Jews they could, Wise, explained, was not simply humanitarian in nature. It was more than just a matter of relieving suffering and death. A major moral obligation was involved, he claimed. The free world would be able to atone, or make up for, its failure to stop Hitler's consolidation of power in the 1930s, which had led to his instigation of both the bloodiest conflict in history and the Holocaust. "Such rescue of the surviving" Jews, Wise maintained, "may in part redeem the world's shame of the years 1933–1939." Throughout those years,

> every manner of nameless crime was committed against our [Jewish] brothers. [I] choose to register my unchanged faith in the deep humanity of the foremost leader of the men in the world today, Franklin D. Roosevelt. [He], along with [Britain's] Prime Minister Churchill, will insist upon the acceleration of the tempo of rescue and take the lead in performing the supremely imperative task of Jewish rescue.[34]

Wise was far from alone in urging quick action to help the threatened European Jews. An American group, the Emergency Committee to Save the Jewish People of Europe, formed midway through the war. In July 1944 its spokesperson, Johan J. Smertenko, sent a letter to Roosevelt. The Allies must bomb the railways leading to the death camps, the letter demanded, "to prevent the transportation of the Hebrew people of these [enemy] countries to Hitler's slaughter houses." In the midst of these attacks, the letter said, at least some Jews would be able to escape and "join the underground resistance forces."[35]

How Would a Rescue Effort Be Justified?

Wise, Smertenko, and others who urged Allied leaders to save at least some Jews from certain death in Nazi camps were sorely disappointed when no concerted rescue operations material-

President Franklin D. Roosevelt (left) confers with Prime Minister Winston Churchill (right) in 1941. American Jews implored the leaders of the United States and Great Britain to step up their efforts to help Europe's Jews.

ized during the war's final year. But the debate over whether such operations would have been worth the effort did not end when the war did. Many experts remain convinced that the free world failed in its moral duty to save at least some of the victims of the death camps. In 1979, for instance, American historian Henry L. Feingold proposed that "thousands of Hungarian and Slovakian Jews might have been saved [in 1944] had the American 15th Air Force, stationed in Italy, and already bombing the synthetic oil and rubber works not five miles from the gas chambers [of Auschwitz], been allowed"[36] to bomb the death camp itself.

One question that inevitably arises in this debate is how many Jews needed to be saved in order to justify the rescue operations. Would saving a thousand have made the operations worth the time and effort? Or did the figure need to be higher? The late University of Chicago historian Peter Novick felt that rescue attempts would have been well worth the effort even if the number saved was small. He did some tentative calculations, however, that suggest that the number would not have been small. "A much more energetic program of rescue on all fronts," he wrote, "might have reduced the overall [Jewish death] toll by perhaps 1 percent, conceivably 2 percent."[37] If it was indeed 2 percent, that translates to about 120,000 Jewish lives.

Saving that many lives would easily have justified "military intervention to try to stop the Holocaust," historian Theodore S. Hamerow of the University of Wisconsin says. But even if the number saved had been far fewer, some sort of rescue operation should have been tried, he argues. The reason is "not because of its practical consequences," he continues, "not because of its chances of success." Rather, it should have been done "because of its underlying rightness, its moral significance. To stand by while a monstrous crime was being committed against millions of guiltless, defenseless human beings was a violation of the basic humanitarian ideals of democracy."[38]

> "To stand by while a monstrous crime was being committed against millions of guiltless, defenseless human beings was a violation of the basic humanitarian ideals of democracy."[38]
>
> —University of Wisconsin scholar Theodore S. Hamerow

The Europa Plan

Not only was saving at least some of the otherwise condemned Jews the ethical thing to do, it might not have required expending a lot of military resources and thereby increasing the length of the conflict. Some covert diplomacy and the outlay of a few million dollars might well have saved 1 million or more Jewish lives. This assertion is based on some real negotiations that occurred in 1944 and 1945, a period in which the Allies were tightening the noose, so to speak, around Nazi Germany.

The strange case of the so-called Europa Plan began in mid-1944. Nazi official Dieter Wisliceny secretly approached some Hungarian Jewish leaders. Wisliceny claimed that his boss, high-placed Nazi Adolf Eichmann, was willing to allow 1 million captive Jews to escape to the West. In exchange, the Allies would supply the Nazis with ten thousand trucks and some other vehicles and supplies, which Eichmann declared would be used against the Soviets, not Britain or the United States.

When British and American leaders learned of this offer, they were highly suspicious, as were a number of leading Jews in the resistance. Rudolf Vrba, a Czech Jew who had the distinction of escaping from Auschwitz and later saving thousands of Jewish lives, called it "a clever ruse."[39] Vrba believed that Eichmann and Wisliceny were trying to lull large numbers of Jews into a false sense of security. Supposedly, that would make them easier to handle as they went to their deaths in the camps.

Some historians, though, believe it is highly probable that the Nazis were serious about the Europa Plan. Noted Israeli historian Yehuda Bauer thinks that by 1944 Eichmann and other high-ranking Nazis knew that simultaneously fighting the Soviets in the East and other Allies in the West was a losing proposition. By making deals for Jewish lives, Bauer says, the Nazis might make a separate peace with the West, which might then join with Hitler to fight the Soviets. The Europa Plan, therefore, might compel "the Western powers [to] come to terms with [Nazi] Germany,"[40] Bauer explains.

Unfortunately, no one will ever know whether those million Jews would have survived the war, because the apprehensive Allies did not pursue the deal. But the possibility remains that, in historian Michael R. Marrus's words, some leading Nazis were "ready to abandon the genocidal program in favor of other objectives of a dying regime."[41] Significantly reducing the severity of the Holocaust was therefore at least possible.

The Allies Could Not Have Reduced the Severity of the Holocaust

"The only ways Germany's opponents could have reduced the carnage [of the Holocaust] significantly were for the British and/ or the Soviets to lose the war in 1941 [or] for the Allies to win the conflict in 1942–1943, which was clearly beyond their power."

—Northwestern University scholar Peter Hayes

Peter Hayes, *Why? Explaining the Holocaust.* New York: Norton, 2017, p. 328.

Consider these questions as you read:

1. Do you feel that the Allies' decision not to divert large amounts of resources to save Europe's Jews was justified? Why or why not?
2. If you had been a young adult during World War II, what would you have said at the time to an American who seemed uninterested in the plight of Europe's Jews?
3. Why is isolationism a potentially self-defeating stance for a country to take in a highly interconnected world?

Editor's note: The discussion that follows presents common arguments made in support of this perspective. All arguments are supported by facts, quotes, and examples taken from various sources of the period or present day.

It was never a viable, realistic option for the free world, led by the Allies, to rescue the Jews that the Nazis victimized during the Holocaust. It would have been far too difficult and risky a venture during the global chaos caused by World War II. Furthermore, there was no practical way to save more than a mere handful of the Jews marked for extermination. This unofficial policy of the United States, Britain, and the other major Allies was stated by different government officials at different times.

Not a Practical Project

One of the more articulate expressions of that policy took place in June 1944. John W. Pehle, head of the War Refugee Board, an agency created by Roosevelt to help displaced civilians around the world, wrote a letter to Assistant Secretary of War John J. McCloy. "There is little doubt," Pehle said, "that many [Hungarian] Jews are being sent to the [Nazi] extermination camps."[42] For humanitarian reasons, Pehle said, the Americans and British should bomb the railway lines leading from Hungary to Auschwitz.

In response, McCloy made it plain that he greatly sympathized with the plight of European Jews, yet he indicated that the proposed bombing was unlikely. "The suggested air operation is impracticable," McCloy wrote. It could occur only if the Allies could divert the "considerable air support essential to the success of our forces now engaged in decisive operations." Moreover, even if such air attacks could be mounted, they would "be of such very doubtful efficacy [value] that it would not amount to a practical project."[43] Simply put, McCloy concluded, Allied forces had more pressing missions to accomplish.

> "The positive solution to the problem [of saving Europe's Jews] is the earliest possible victory over Germany."[44]
>
> —US assistant secretary of war John J. McCloy

Later, in November 1944 Pehle sent McCloy another plea, urging him to recommend direct bombing of the Nazi death camps. McCloy answered that the death camps were mostly in Poland and therefore too far away. Fighter bombers stationed in Britain and France lacked the fuel capacity to fly to Poland and back. Heavy bombers could carry enough fuel, he added, but they would require escort fighter planes to guard them, and the risk of losing large numbers of valuable aircraft was too great. "The positive solution to the problem," McCloy said, "is the earliest possible victory over Germany."[44]

Simmering Anti-Semitism

Bombing the death camps was only one of several plans for rescuing Jews that were proposed during the conflict. Various individuals and groups suggested others, among them secretly bargaining with Nazi leaders to release Jews in exchange for money or military supplies.

None of these plans would have worked any better than the bombing one, in part because of the cruel and sad truth that not enough people in the West cared enough about the plight of Europe's Jews. Indeed, Europe was not the only hotbed of anti-Semitism in the world. Even in democracies like Britain and the United States, there were too many feelings of distrust for and hostility toward Jews.

These feelings, like so many others associated with blind prejudice, were based on fear and ignorance. Wherever they lived, most Jews tended to adapt well to existing society. They were hard workers who valued knowledge and talent and made sure their children were well educated. As a result, far out of proportion to their numbers, Jews often did well in business and rose to high positions in their communities. People like Hitler and his Nazi thugs could not accept that Jews possessed constructive qualities and therefore assumed they got ahead by greed, cheating, and other underhanded means. Although few in the West expressed such ugly ideas as overtly as the Nazis did, distrust of Jews ran deep in some circles in most Western countries.

Most of the government officials in Roosevelt's administration were not explicitly anti-Semitic, but they were well aware that fear and dislike of Jews frequently simmered beneath the surface of American society. These leaders worried about what Americans might think if the United States and other Allies appeared to play favorites with foreign-born Jews by trying to rescue them. Many US politicians worried that such rescues would play right into Hitler's hands. As scholar Theodore S. Hamerow puts it, the Nazis would be sure to frame Allied rescue attempts of Jews "as proof that the Allies were following the orders of cunning Jewish manipulators and wire-pullers." Moreover, he explains,

all the traditional ethnic biases of the Old World, which the war had clearly not diminished, were bound to be intensified. Worst of all, how would the American public react to reports that American airmen were risking their lives in an attempt to save some of the Jews imprisoned in the death camps? It was obvious that direct military intervention to stop the Holocaust could have a serious adverse effect on the war effort. It would be best not to try it.[45]

Leave America Out of It?

Anti-Semitism was not the only reason that the free world did not seriously contemplate rescuing large numbers of Jews from Nazi death camps. Fear and distrust of foreigners in general was also a factor. Here again, what was happening in the United States during the war reflected the situation in a number of other Allied nations as well. In the years between the two world wars, isolationist feelings were strong among many Americans. Typically, isolationists held that Europeans, Asians, and other foreigners should deal with their own problems and leave America out of it. Although isolationism weakened in the United States after the country entered World War II, a potent streak of it remained in some social and political quarters.

It was not just that many of the victims of Hitler's death camps were Jews, therefore. Whether they were Jews, Slavs, gypsies, or others, first and foremost they were all foreigners. One modern scholar sums up this attitude held by a number of American leaders during the war, saying they suspected

> that members of the Jewish community were trying to persuade the American government to use its diplomatic, financial, and military resources to save their [fellow Jews] in Europe. Those efforts had to be resisted. [The] chief concern of the American government should be the welfare of the American people. This view was shared by most of the politicians and officials in Washington. They preferred not to express it openly, since that might leave them vulnerable to charges of heartlessness and bigotry. But from time to time . . . there was no mistaking how they felt.[46]

Indeed, one instance in which an American official *did* express how he really felt about the issue occurred in November 1943. After one of his colleagues introduced a resolution calling on the government to help the Jews in the death camps, Representative Karl E. Mundt of South Dakota registered his disapproval. "As a general policy for this country," he stated, "it is not good practice for us to [single out the Jews or other] groups of people by their religion . . . for special consideration [because] that would be treading a pretty dangerous path. It is sort of doing the Hitler thing in reverse."[47]

Harsh but Necessary

Underlying these feelings of discomfort with foreigners was a real fear in the United States that huge numbers of European refugees, Jews and non-Jews alike, would flood the country. Most US and British leaders agreed with an assessment of the potential refugee problem compiled by Britain's Royal Institute of International Affairs. "The immediate need," it stated in part, "is to prevent any further movement of European Jewry from becoming a refugee movement." For a while, at least, "harsh though it is,"[48] the institute maintained that the West must close down its borders to any further European refugees.

> "The immediate need is to prevent any further movement of European Jewry from becoming a refugee movement."[48]
>
> —Britain's Royal Institute of International Affairs

Clearly, the attitude of a majority of Allied politicians and military officials was that the potential refugee crisis was better left to sort out when the war was over. For the moment, the cost of handling and resettling the millions of Jews and other Europeans who wanted to flee to the West would impede the ongoing effort to achieve victory over the Nazis. Rescuing the Jews from the death camps—even if it were logistically possible—would only create an enormous refugee problem. In early 1943 the British Foreign and Commonwealth Office summed up this opinion in a telegraphed message to Washington, DC. "The blunt truth," the message stated,

> is that the whole complex of human problems raised by the present German domination of Europe [can] only be dealt with completely by an Allied victory, and any step calculated to prejudice this is not in the interest of the Jews in Europe. The only real remedy for the consistent Nazi policy of racial and religious persecution lies in an Allied victory. Every resource must be bent towards this supreme object.[49]

Chapter Five

Were the Nuremburg Trials Legally and Morally Justified?

The Nuremburg Trials Were Legally and Morally Justified

- In response to the mass murders the Nazis carried out, the victors—the Allies—had a duty to prosecute the perpetrators in a manner befitting the huge scale of their crime.
- The Nuremberg Trials did not legally violate Germany's sovereignty as a nation because the German government had collapsed at the end of the war.
- The trials were morally justified in that they educated the world about the enormity of the Nazis' crimes and thereby laid the foundations for a safer future for humanity.

The Debate at a Glance

The Nuremburg Trials Were Not Legally or Morally Justified

- The trials applied a blatant form of victors' justice, in which the war's winners dictated all the legal rules and procedures.
- The prosecutors charged the defendants with war crimes that the Allies themselves had sometimes committed.
- In charging the surviving Nazis with crimes against humanity, the Nuremberg tribunal subverted a long-standing legal principle that defendants could not be charged for crimes that were not previously recognized as crimes.

The Nuremburg Trials Were Legally and Morally Justified

"[The Nuremberg tribunal] gives both the world today and the world tomorrow a chance to see the justice of the Allied cause and the wickedness of the Nazis', and [sets] a firm foundation for a future world order wherein individuals will know that if they embark on schemes of aggression or murder or torture or persecution they will be severely dealt with by the world."

—US federal judge Charles E. Wyzanski

Charles E. Wyzanski, "Nuremberg: A Fair Trial? A Dangerous Precedent," *Atlantic*, April 1946. www.theatlantic.com.

Consider these questions as you read:

1. Do you think victors' justice is morally acceptable? Explain why or why not.
2. Why did the Nazi perpetration of the Holocaust make World War II different from all prior conflicts?
3. Did Germany learn a major lesson from its defeat and the Nuremberg Trials? Explain your answer, pointing out certain customs and laws the Germans later instituted.

Editor's note: The discussion that follows presents common arguments made in support of this perspective. All arguments are supported by facts, quotes, and examples taken from various sources of the period or present day.

In November 1945 the Allies began to bring the surviving Nazi leaders to trial in Nuremberg, Germany. On behalf of the twenty-six nations making up the Allies, the four strongest and most influential—the United States, Britain, France, and the Soviet Union—set up the court, prosecuted the accused, and supplied the judges. In all, twenty-four Nazi men and six German organizations were indicted.

There were four principal charges. The first was conspiracy to wage aggressive war; the second was actually waging aggressive war, also called committing crimes against peace; the third was committing war crimes; and the fourth was committing crimes against humanity. Each of the four charges incorporated a number of subcharges related to it. For example, the third main charge—committing war crimes—included the reckless destruction of entire cities and towns, theft of private property, taking and murdering hostages, and causing devastation that was not militarily necessary. Viewed in their entirety, the charges marked the first time in history that the world community sought to punish a group of individuals for starting a war and conducting it in an inhumane fashion.

Counsels for the Nazi defendants tried to clear their clients by arguing in effect that the trials themselves were not morally justified. Nor were they even legal under international law, the counsels claimed. Although one might expect such audacious arguments from the defense, the Nazis' lawyers were not the only ones who made them. A number of American, British, and other Western judges and legal experts agreed that the trials were not justified and said so in various newspaper articles and essays in the months and years following the war.

The Victors' Brand of Justice?

All of those naysayers were completely incorrect in making such assertions. The Nuremberg Trials were totally reasonable. First, they were ethically justified; and second, they were perfectly legal under laws that had developed in civilized nations over the course of many centuries. That they were morally justified is perfectly plain when one examines the frequent charge that they were a blatant example of victors' justice. That term has long been applied to cases in which the winners of a conflict spitefully enact their vengeance and retaliation on the losers.

For example, numerous German writers and politicians accused the Allies of applying victors' justice to Germany after it lost

World War I. In the Treaty of Versailles, Britain, France, and the United States severely reduced Germany's armed forces, rendering it largely helpless, and demanded enormous reparations— payments of money to the winners. Making those payments subsequently crippled Germany's economy for close to a decade. Thus, there is perhaps a case to be made that the Allies did force a sort of victors' justice on Germany after that first global conflict.

But the same cannot be said about the way the Allies handled the situation following the end of World War II. That putting the leading Nazis on trial to pay for their war crimes was justified is easily proved by the magnitude of those crimes. Never before in human history had a nation staged so many unprovoked attacks on its neighbors and committed so many horrendous atrocities during the course of the fighting. The killing of some 6 million Jews in the Holocaust, as terrible as it was, was only the proverbial tip of the iceberg in the list of the Nazis' grievous misdeeds. Moreover, the world needed to respond to this unprecedented slaughter in a manner befitting its enormity. Scholar Jan Schnitzer aptly sums up this view, saying:

> "Although it was the victorious Allies who presided over the vanquished Germans, the Nuremberg Trials in my opinion cannot be seen as vengeance of the victors."[50]
>
> —Scholar Jan Schnitzer

In respect to the given circumstances, [the Nuremberg Trials were] an exceptional and admirable way to deal with those responsible for [war crimes]. Nuremberg set a precedent for international law, and [made clear] once and for all that no jurist should ever again just apply the given law of one's country without paying respect to the most basic moral principles of humankind. [Therefore,] although it was the victorious Allies who presided over the vanquished Germans, the Nuremberg Trials in my opinion cannot be seen as vengeance of the victors.[50]

Germany's Sovereignty Violated?

Another common criticism of the Nuremberg Trials, especially within Germany itself, has been that these international tribunals violated Germany's sovereignty, or independent autonomy as a separate nation. According to this view, the Allies had no right to try German citizens. Instead, the war's victors should have let the Germans themselves prosecute and punish the surviving Nazi leaders.

This argument is bogus for two reasons. First, at the close of the war, Germany did not possess traditional national sovereignty because the German state no longer existed. National Socialism—the formal name of the Nazi movement—had long since cannibalized Germany's government. Hitler and his Nazi thugs had "infiltrated all areas of life in Germany so deeply that its end caused the complete collapse of German society,"[51] Schnitzer argues.

The second reason that the Nuremberg Trials did not violate Germany's sovereignty is that in 1945 German courts and judges

Prominent Nazi leaders, accused of committing war crimes and facing other charges, appear in court during the 1945 Nuremberg Trials. Many experts say the magnitude of the crimes committed by the Nazis more than justified the trials.

were not trustworthy enough to administer justice to the surviving Nazis. Many of those judges had been appointed by Nazi leaders. Others had rubber-stamped Nazi abuses of the country's legal system and were therefore complicit in the Nazis' war crimes. These court officials could not be expected to hand down fair and impartial decisions in the punishment of those same Nazis. It was therefore up to Allied prosecutors and judges to step in and administer justice to those who perpetrated the conflict and murdered millions of innocent Jews and others.

The Allies' legal right to do so was based on the precedents of peace treaties that had ended many earlier wars. The leading American legal minds, including several members of the Supreme Court, examined this issue in the months following the war's end. Widely respected US federal judge Charles E. Wyzanski summarized their overall conclusion. "There can be no doubt," he stated,

> of the legal right of this nation, prior to the signing of a peace treaty, to use a military tribunal for the purpose of trying and punishing a German if [in] occupied territory he murdered a Polish civilian, or tortured a Czech, or raped a Frenchwoman, or robbed a Belgian. Moreover, there is no doubt of the [Nuremberg] military tribunal's parallel right to try and to punish a German if he has murdered, tortured, or maltreated a prisoner of war.[52]

Learning from History

Another way the Nuremberg Trials were morally justified was that they were in a very real sense a history lesson that absolutely needed to be taught. There is a groundswell of academic and political opinion that believes the principal purpose of the Nuremberg Trials was not to punish Nazi leaders but rather to provide a history lesson to educate people, especially the German population, about the Nazis' crimes.

Robert Kempner, one of the prosecutors at Nuremberg, articulated this crucial point when he memorably described the trials as "the greatest history seminar ever held in the history of the world."[53] The Nuremberg Trials, he went on, were more than anything else intended to reveal to the German people the nature and brutality of the Nazis' war crimes. It was hoped that this would have two outcomes. First, it would instill a potent sense of shame in the German people that would keep them from turning the Nazi leaders into martyrs.

Second, it was hoped that the history lesson provided by the trials would deter future generations of Germans and other Europeans from the kind of war-mongering Hitler and his cronies had engaged in. Henry Stimson, who served as US secretary of war during the conflict, spoke to that point. He said that the trials were created "for the purpose of prevention and not for vengeance."[54]

> "[The trials were] the greatest history seminar ever held in the history of the world."[53]
>
> —Nuremberg prosecutor Robert Kempner

Another positive and welcome way the trials held by the Allies affected the future was to establish an important legal and judicial precedent for the global community of nations. In particular, the Nuremberg tribunals became a model for later international courts of various kinds. An outstanding example is the International Criminal Court, established in 1998 and headquartered in The Hague, Netherlands. A spokesperson for the organization describes its mission, saying that it "investigates and, where warranted, tries individuals charged with the gravest crimes of concern to the international community: genocide, war crimes, crimes against humanity and the crime of aggression."[55] If for no other reason, therefore, the Nuremberg Trials were justified because they laid the foundation for a safer, more humane global society. In the words of the late German-born British legal scholar Georg Schwarzenberger, the trials and the later international courts they inspired proved that "when there is a will amongst the world powers to cooperate, a common denominator for such joint effort can be found."[56]

The Nuremburg Trials Were Not Legally or Morally Justified

"At Nuremberg, [the] standards of 'justice' applied only to the vanquished. The four powers that sat in judgment were themselves guilty of many of the very crimes they accused the German leaders of committing."

—American historian Mark Weber

Mark Weber, "The Nuremberg Trials and the Holocaust," *Journal of Historical Review*, 2002.

Consider these questions as you read:

1. Do you think the Allies were justified in firebombing German cities, killing thousands of civilians, to speed the end of the war? Why or why not?
2. In your view, are there other effective methods of exacting justice from a defeated nation besides putting its leaders on trial? Explain your answer.
3. Should it be automatic that the losers of a war be put on trial by the victors? Why or why not?

Editor's note: The discussion that follows presents common arguments made in support of this perspective. All arguments are supported by facts, quotes, and examples taken from various sources of the period or present day.

The Nuremberg Trials, which began in late 1945 in the wake of Germany's defeat in World War II, have rightly been criticized over the years as being on questionable legal and moral grounds at best. On the one hand, they were a cynical display of old-fashioned victors' justice. On the other, they breached various kinds of ethics, including, at one point, medical ones, and violated some of the oldest legal principles that Western civilization had developed over the course of many centuries.

Specific condemnations of the Nuremberg Trials have been numerous and at times scathing. US Supreme Court justice Harlan Fiske Stone, an august legal expert, famously called them a "high-grade lynching affair."[57] Similarly, distinguished British historian Richard Overy dismisses the Nuremberg tribunal as largely "a political act, agreed at the level of diplomacy, and motivated by political interests."[58] American historian Mark Weber agrees. "The Nuremberg enterprise violated ancient and fundamental principles of justice," he states.

> The victorious Allies acted as prosecutor, judge, and executioner of the German leaders. The charges were created especially for the occasion, and were applied only to the vanquished. Defeated, starving, prostrate Germany was, however, in no position to oppose whatever the Allied occupation powers demanded. As even some leading Allied figures privately acknowledged at the time, the Nuremberg trials were organized not to dispense impartial justice, but for political purposes.[59]

War Crimes on Both Sides?

That the Allies exacted traditional victors' justice at Nuremberg is clearly demonstrated by the evidence. Numerous well-known individuals pointed it out during and after the trials, including one of the defendants, Hermann Goering, commander of Hitler's air force, the Luftwaffe. "The victor will always be the judge and the vanquished the accused,"[60] he remarked upon learning that he and his colleagues would be prosecuted.

It would be easy to dismiss this comment as worthless because it came from a leading Nazi. Yet many prominent figures in the Allied camp said essentially the same thing. Widely respected US senator Robert A. Taft was one of them. In a speech delivered in October 1946, he stated:

The trial of the vanquished by the victors cannot be impartial no matter how it is hedged about with the forms of justice. About this whole judgment there is the spirit of vengeance, and vengeance is seldom justice. [It] will be a blot on the American record which we will long regret. In these trials we have accepted [using] government policy and not justice—with little relation to Anglo-Saxon heritage.[61]

By "Anglo-Saxon heritage," Taft meant the large-scale collection of Western legal concepts built on the foundation of the Magna Carta, which was created in 1215. Implicit in this imposing body of law is the idea that the strong must not take advantage of the weak simply because they can. In the context of the Nuremberg tribunal, the war's victors were the strong and its losers the weak.

> "The trial of the vanquished by the victors cannot be impartial."[61]
>
> —US senator Robert A. Taft

Operating from that position of strength, Taft explained, the Allies could dictate what was and was not to be considered a war crime. Moreover, they could conveniently ignore the fact that at least some of those so-called crimes were expected behavior by combatants on both sides in the conflict. Indeed, British social critic Henry Fairlie correctly observed, "If the victors were to 'try' the vanquished for war crimes, then they should try themselves for often committing the same crimes."[62]

This point was well taken. None of the Allies faced criminal responsibility for war crimes, despite the fact that at the height of the conflict they had carried out some of the same transgressions the Nazis had. Many historians, statesmen and stateswomen, and other expert observers cited the example of American planes firebombing German cities and in the process incinerating hun-

Hermann Goering, the commander of the Luftwaffe, faces his accusers during the Nuremberg Trials. Goering doubted he would receive a fair trial because he was on the losing side; this perspective was also expressed by some prominent US officials.

dreds of thousands of civilians. Also, while the Nazis had instigated the Holocaust against the Jews, the Soviets had massacred thousands of Polish soldiers in the Katyn Forest. There was also the US use of a new superweapon—the atomic bomb—on two Japanese cities, again resulting in the slaughter of hundreds of thousands of civilians.

A Question of Medical Ethics

Atomic bombs and mass murder were not the only factors that needed to be considered during the Nuremberg Trials. In one of these court proceedings, twenty-three Nazi doctors were tried for and convicted of acts of torture and barbarism during medical experiments on Jews and other captives. One Nazi physician, Karl Gebhardt, for example, had broken prisoners' legs with hammers, without administering painkillers, and then tried various remedies, all to find the best ways of treating wounded German soldiers. He had also cut off captives' arms or legs (also without anesthetic) and attempted to transplant them onto German soldiers who had lost limbs in battle.

As gruesome as these experiments were, counsels for the Nazi defendants argued that the Allies had performed similar ones. In particular, the defense singled out an experiment performed during the war by American doctors on prisoners in Stateville Prison in Joliet, Illinois. More than four hundred inmates were infected with malaria, and various medicines were administered to them, in some cases in doses high enough to be potentially toxic.

According to the *Chicago Daily Tribune*, "None of the volunteering convicts died but many were made violently ill as a result of their infection with [a potent form of] malaria and subsequent treatment with drugs then in the experimental stage."[63] Other sources said that at least one prisoner died. But even if there were no deaths, numerous medical experts in the West questioned whether it was ethical to conduct such experiments on captives. What Nazi doctors did during the war was undoubtedly worse than what happened at Stateville Prison, but only by degree. The Nuremberg defendants were right to argue that the Allies charged them with committing the same crime their own doctors had committed.

Subverting Justice?

Possibly the most compelling legal criticism of the Nuremberg Trials, one widely voiced at the time and ever since, is that it violated a fundamental principle of law—generally referred to as *nullum crimen sine lege*. Literally translated from Latin, it means "no crime without a law." In actual practice, it consists of holding someone accountable for acts that had not when committed been designated as crimes.

At Nuremberg, the fourth and last charge against the Nazi defendants—committing crimes against humanity, is the one that flew in the face of long-established legal procedures by ignoring the principle of *nullum crimen sine lege*. In the words of a mid-twentieth-century legal scholar, the use of the crimes against humanity charge "constituted a unilateral [one-sided] act of the Allied Powers committed without regard to the long established practice of states or the generally accepted rules of international law."[64]

The main reason that the Nuremberg defendants should not have been charged with crimes against humanity is that this was a new "crime," one largely manufactured by the Allies in the wake of their victory over Nazi Germany. At the time that the Nazis committed various wartime acts, some of those acts were not widely viewed as crimes against the human race, which is in itself an overly broad legal definition. It is true that the Nazi leaders were aware that committing mass murder is morally wrong. So when they sent millions of Jews and others to their deaths in concentration camps, they were guilty of a crime. The question is how such a crime should be defined and labeled. To call it a "war crime" would be appropriate. But because "crimes against humanity" was not a legal concept before World War II, the Nuremberg defendants should not have been charged with it.

Many theories have been proposed to explain why the prosecutors did employ that charge. Some suggest it was a desperate attempt by the Allies to make the case that the Nazis had been more heinous and reprehensible than any other warmongers in history. That way there would be few objections to executing the

> "It cannot be claimed that [the Nuremberg tribunal] was a trial comparable with those under more stable systems of law. It was, rather, a legalistic means of eliminating the Nazi leaders."[65]
>
> —Harvard University legal scholar Judith N. Shklar

surviving Nazi leaders. If so, this strategy was of at least questionable legality. The late noted Harvard University legal scholar Judith N. Shklar perceptively noted, "It cannot be claimed that this was a trial comparable with those under more stable systems of law. It was, rather, a legalistic means of eliminating the Nazi leaders."[65] No one disputes that the Nuremberg defendants were disreputable individuals who deserved to be punished. But by trumping up an unprecedented charge designed to make sure these men would not escape justice, the Allied tribunal itself subverted both justice and the law.

Source Notes

Chapter One: A Brief History of the Holocaust

1. Jewish Virtual Library, "The Holocaust: An Introductory History." www.jewishvirtuallibrary.org.
2. Quoted in Office of the US Chief of Counsel for Prosecution of Axis Criminality, ed., *Nazi Conspiracy and Aggression*, vol. 4. Washington, DC: U.S. Government Printing Office, 1946, pp. 789–90.
3. Holocaust Teacher Resource Center, "Oh, No, It Can't Be," 2018. http://www.holocaust-trc.org.

Chapter Two: Was Adolf Hitler the Primary Force Behind the Holocaust?

4. Theodore S. Hamerow, *Why We Watched: Europe, America, and the Holocaust*. New York: Norton, 2008, p. 6.
5. Adolf Hitler, *Mein Kampf*. Boston: Houghton Mifflin, 1969, pp. 295–96.
6. Hitler, *Mein Kampf*, p. 296.
7. Quoted in Norman H. Baynes, ed., *The Speeches of Adolph Hitler*. New York: Fertig, 1969, p. 735.
8. Quoted in Peter Longerich, *Holocaust: The Nazi Persecution and Murder of the Jews*. New York: Oxford University Press, 2010, p. 289.
9. Quoted in Jeremy Noakes and Geoffrey Pridham, eds., *Nazism, 1919–1945*, vol. 3: *Foreign Policy, War and Racial Extermination: A Documentary Reader*. Exeter, UK: University of Exeter Press, 2001, pp. 515–16.
10. Quoted in Jewish Virtual Library, "Joseph Goebbels: On the Jewish Question." www.jewishvirtuallibrary.org.
11. Quoted in Lorraine Boissoneault, "The First Moments of Hitler's Final Solution," *Smithsonian*, December 12, 2016. www.smithsonianmag.com.
12. Quoted in Peter Crawford, "An Englishman at the Court of the Kaiser," *Occult History of the Third Reich* (blog), 2012. http://thirdreichocculthistory.blogspot.com.

13. Vera Laska, *Women in the Resistance and in the Holocaust: The Voices of Eyewitnesses*. Westport, CT: Greenwood, 1983, p. xiii.
14. Laurence Rees, *The Holocaust: A New History*. New York: Public Affairs, 2017, p. 429.
15. Michael R. Marrus, *The Holocaust in History*. Hanover, NH: University Press of New England, 1987, p. 42.
16. Richard Rhodes, *Masters of Death: The SS and the Invention of the Holocaust*. New York: Knopf, 2002, p. 35.
17. René Girard, *Things Hidden Since the Foundation of the World*. Stanford, CA: Stanford University Press, 1987, p. 24.

Chapter Three: Could Europe's Jews Have Put Up More Resistance to Nazi Aggression?
18. Raul Hilberg, *The Destruction of the European Jews*, vol. 3. New York: Holmes and Meier, 1985, p. 1030.
19. Quoted in Leo Alexander, "War Crimes and Their Motivation," *Journal of Criminal Law and Criminology*, 1948–1949, p. 315.
20. Hilberg, *The Destruction of the European Jews*, p. 1034.
21. Quoted in Peter Hayes, *Why? Explaining the Holocaust*. New York: Norton, 2017, p. 186.
22. Quoted in Hayes, *Why? Explaining the Holocaust*, p. 186.
23. Eric Gartman, "Resistance to the Holocaust: Not like Sheep to the Slaughter: Jewish Resistance in the Holocaust," Jewish Virtual Library. www.jewishvirtuallibrary.org.
24. Hilberg, *The Destruction of the European Jews*, pp. 1038–39.
25. Lyn Smith, *Remembering: Voices of the Holocaust*. New York: Carroll and Graf, 2006, p. 184.
26. Laska, *Women in the Resistance and in the Holocaust*, pp. 4–5.
27. Quoted in Jacob Sloan, ed. and trans., *Notes from the Warsaw Ghetto: The Journal of Emmanuel Ringelblum*. New York: Schocken, 1974, p. 295.
28. Marrus, *The Holocaust in History*, p. 138.
29. Doreen Rappaport, *Beyond Courage: The Untold Story of Jewish Resistance During the Holocaust*. Somerville, MA: Candlewick, 2012, p. 169.
30. Longerich, *Holocaust*, pp. 377–78.

31. Quoted in J. Yalovitser, "Zog nit keynmol Jewish Partisans Tribute Warsaw Ghetto Uprising 1943," *Songs of My People*. www.songsofmypeople.com.

Chapter Four: Could the Allies Have Reduced the Severity of the Holocaust?

32. Hamerow, *Why We Watched*, p. 390.
33. Stephen S. Wise, *As I See It*. New York: Jewish Opinion, 1944, p. 77.
34. Wise, *As I See It*, pp. 77–78.
35. Quoted in Hamerow, *Why We Watched*, p. 392.
36. Henry L. Feingold, "Who Shall Bear the Guilt for the Holocaust: The Human Dilemma," *American Jewish History*, March 1979, p. 271.
37. Peter Novick, *The Holocaust in American Life*. Boston: Little, Brown, 1999, p. 58.
38. Hamerow, *Why We Watched*, p. 392.
39. Quoted in Martin Gilbert, *Auschwitz and the Allies*. New York: Holt, Rinehart, and Winston, 1981, p. 205.
40. Yehuda Bauer, "Genocide: Was It the Nazis' Original Plan?," *Annals of the American Academy of Political and Social Science*, July 1980, p. 44.
41. Marrus, *The Holocaust in History*, p. 188.
42. Quoted in Hamerow, *Why We Watched*, p. 404.
43. Quoted in Hamerow, *Why We Watched*, p. 404.
44. Quoted in Hamerow, *Why We Watched*, p. 404.
45. Hamerow, *Why We Watched*, p. 403.
46. Hamerow, *Why We Watched*, p. 397.
47. US House of Representatives, Committee on International Relations, *Selected Executive Session Hearings of the Committee, 1943–1950*, vol. 2, part 2. Washington DC: Government Printing Office, 1976, p. 16.
48. John H. Simpson, *Refugees: Preliminary Report of a Survey*. London: Royal Institute of International Affairs, 1938, p. 193.
49. Quoted in Bernard Wasserstein, *Britain and the Jews of Europe, 1939–1945*. London: Leicester University Press, 1999, p. 219.

Chapter Five: Were the Nuremburg Trials Legally and Morally Justified?

50. Jan Schnitzer, *The Nuremberg Justice Trial, 1947—Vengeance of the Victors*. Wellington, New Zealand: Victoria University of Wellington, 2010, p. 18.
51. Schnitzer, *The Nuremberg Justice Trial, 1947*, p. 38.
52. Charles E. Wyzanski, "Nuremberg: A Fair Trial? A Dangerous Precedent," *Atlantic*, April 1946. www.theatlantic.com.
53. Quoted in Lawrence Douglas, *The Memory of Judgment: Making Law and History in the Trials of the Holocaust*. New Haven, CT: Yale University Press, 2001, p. 2.
54. Quoted in Gary J. Bass, *Stay the Hand of Vengeance: The Politics of War Crimes Tribunals*. Princeton, NJ: Princeton University Press, 2000, p. 157.
55. International Criminal Court, "About." www.icc-cpi.int.
56. Georg Schwarzenberger, "The Judgment of Nuremberg," in *Perspectives on the Nuremberg Trial*, ed. Guenael Mettraux. Oxford: Oxford University Press, 2008, p. 188.
57. Quoted in Douglas, *The Memory of Judgment*, p. 49.
58. Richard Overy, "The Nuremberg Trials: International Law in the Making," in *From Nuremberg to The Hague: The Future of International Criminal Justice*, ed. Phillippe Sands. Cambridge: Cambridge University Press, 2003, p. 29.
59. Mark Weber, "The Nuremberg Trials and the Holocaust," *Journal of Historical Review*, vol. 12, no. 2, 2002. www.vho.org.
60. Quoted in J.E. Persico, *Nuremberg: Infamy on Trial*. New York: Penguin, 1994, p. 83.
61. Quoted in Weber, "The Nuremberg Trials and the Holocaust."
62. Henry Fairlie, "How the Good War Went Bad," *New Republic*, May 20, 1985, p. 18.
63. Quoted in *Prison Culture* (blog), "Prisoners and Medical Experimentation: Willing Bodies?," February 2, 2012. www.usprisonculture.com.
64. F.B. Schick, "The Nuremberg Trial and the International Law of the Future," *American Journal of International Law*, vol. 41, 1947, p. 770.
65. Judith N. Shklar, *Legalism: Laws, Morals, and Political Trials*. Cambridge, MA: Harvard University Press, 1964, p. 155.

For Further Research

Books

Sharon Kangisser and Eva Fogelman, *Children in the Holocaust and Its Aftermath*. New York: Berghahn, 2017.

Zoe Lowery and James Norton, *The Nazi Regime and the Holocaust*. New York: Rosen, 2016.

Alexander Macdonald, *The Nuremberg Trials: The Nazis Brought to Justice*. London: Arcturus, 2015.

Don Nardo, *Nazi War Criminals*. San Diego: ReferencePoint, 2016.

Paul Roland, *Life in the Third Reich: Daily Life in Nazi Germany, 1933–1945*. London: Arcturus, 2015.

Marilyn Shimon, *First One In, Last One Out: Auschwitz Survivor 31321*. Charleston, SC: Amazon Digital Services, 2016.

David Weiss, *The Unblazed Trail: How Holocaust Survivors and Perpetrators Escaped Europe*. Charleston, SC: Amazon Digital Services, 2017.

Internet Sources

Maggie Astor, "The Holocaust Is Fading from Memory, Survey Finds," *New York Times*, April 12, 2018. www.nytimes.com/2018/04/12/us/holocaust-education.html.

Larry Bernard, "Historian Examines U.S. Ethics in Nuremberg Medical Trial Tactics," *Cornell Chronicle*, December 5, 1996. http://news.cornell.edu/stories/1996/12/historian-examines-us-ethics-nuremberg-medical-trial-tactics.

Edith Birkin, "Life in the Ghetto: Dreadful, Dreadful Smell," Voices of the Holocaust, British Library. www.bl.uk/learning/histcitizen/voices/testimonies/ghettos/dreadful/lifeinghetto.html.

History Place, "Hitler's Book, *Mein Kampf*," 1996. www.historyplace.com/worldwar2/riseofhitler/kampf.htm.

Ruth Schuster, "Holocaust Movies: 18 of the Best Beyond *Schindler's List*," *Haaretz* (Tel Aviv, Israel), April 11, 2018. www .haaretz.com/jewish/holocaust-remembrance-day/holocaust -movies-17-of-the-best-films-beyond-schindler-s-list-1.5237230.

Alan Taylor, "World War II: The Holocaust," *Atlantic*, October 2011. www.theatlantic.com/photo/2011/10/world-war-ii-the-holo caust/100170.

Websites

The Holocaust, History (www.history.com/topics/world-war-ii /the-holocaust). This useful brief introduction to the enormous subject of the Holocaust contains links to relevant topics such as Adolf Hitler, the Beer Hall Putsch, Palestine, Auschwitz, and the Nuremberg Trials.

Holocaust Encyclopedia (www.ushmm.org/learn/holocaust -encyclopedia). The US Holocaust Memorial Museum offers an excellent and comprehensive online resource. This authoritative site includes links to a wide variety of Holocaust-related topics.

The Holocaust: The "Final Solution," Jewish Virtual Library (www.jewishvirtuallibrary.org/the-quot-final-solution-quot). The Jewish Virtual Library calls itself a go-to source on the topics of Judaism, Israel, and the Holocaust. This excellent site contains numerous links to topics related to the Nazis' implementation of the Final Solution.

A People's History of the Holocaust and Genocide, Remem ber.org (http://remember.org). This outstanding free online service, established in 1995, provides numerous links to all sorts of Holocaust-related topics, including eyewitness accounts by survivors.

Index

Note: Boldface page numbers indicate illustrations.

About the Author

Historian and award-winning author Don Nardo has written numerous books for young adults about World War II, Nazism, and the Holocaust. These include volumes on Pearl Harbor, the war in the Pacific, the Nazis' rise to power, Nazi concentration camps, and biographies of Adolf Hitler and Franklin D. Roosevelt. Nardo, who also composes and arranges orchestral music, lives with his wife, Christine, in Massachusetts.